Prayers to Sta

By **David O'Malley** SDB

DON BOSCO

All readings based on Scripture have been paraphrased, references are given as indications of source.

ISBN 0-9548388-0-7

Other books by David O'Malley
**PRAYERS TO CLOSE THE DAY
ORDINARY WAYS
TRUST THE ROAD
VIA LUCIS**

Details of these books are given on the website

www.don-bosco-publications.co.uk

and they can be purchased there

DON BOSCO

Introduction

The Vatican Council reminded us that, *Morning and Evening Prayer are the two hinges on which the Prayer of the Church turns.* The reflection on life, alongside the words of scripture, has been a daily practice in the Church since earliest times. This book continues that tradition, offering a simple form of prayer for individual or communal use at the start of the day.

The structure of the prayer is simple. It begins with the Sign of the Cross and a greeting. An offering of the day is made, followed by a brief pause indicated by this symbol, 📖. The Choral Prayer is said slowly, and where two or more are gathered, it can be said by alternating voices. A brief meditation is provided each day, to be read quietly or read aloud in groups. There is then a chance to reflect on the day ahead in the light of scripture.

The Benedictus and the Lord's Prayer are included each day, as a link to the traditional Office of the Church. The final prayer has been based on the official Prayers of the Church for each Sunday of the year. Finally, there is a phrase offered for each day. This can easily be remembered, and repeated, like a mantra, linking us back to the prayer that started our day. The language throughout the book has been adapted to make it immediately available to those of us who may not have a strong background in regular prayer and scripture reading.

This book is presented as a partner volume to *Prayers to Close the Day.* It is offered as a way of prayer for busy people. It is also offered as a resource to Christian communities who would like to start their day with a simple form of prayer. It can also serve as an occasional alternative to the full Office of the Church for religious communities and parishes.

So where is the good of being caught up into God's loving prayer, when our activities are trapped in the love of earthly and shallow concerns?

St Francis de Sales

✠ **In the name of the Father, and of the Son, and of the Holy Spirit.**

Greeting
>Peace be in this new day,
>peace of heart and mind,
>peace with the past, peace with the future.
>
>May the peace of Christ make a home in my heart,
>may it disarm anger and calm all fear today,
>may it settle in my soul and stay.

Offering
>Lord, I offer you this day with all the promise and uncertainty it contains. I offer you all my fears and hopes for the day. Be the peace at the centre of my life today. Be the hope that survives each event. Be with me in all that happens.
>📖

Choral Prayer
Based on John 20:19

It was Sunday and the doors were closed in fear
when Jesus came and stood among his disciples.

Jesus gave them peace to calm their fears
and showed them his wounded hands and feet.

Peace be with you Jesus said again
calling them into the way of Risen life.

He breathed on them. The Spirit moved in their hearts
the Spirit of peace and new beginnings.

Happy are those who have not seen
yet clearly see with the eyes of faith.

Glory be to the Father...

Meditation

We live for only six hundred and fifty thousand hours. Like a morning mist, our individual lives seem to come and go with little importance and much frustration. But peace becomes possible when we remember that the morning mist of our lives is the breath of God. We are caught up into God's own life, not just as individuals, but as an inspired people, at the heart of history. All will be well.

The Day Ahead

Where will peace be felt strongly today?

📖

What thoughts will keep me focussed and peaceful?

📖

Where am I at risk of losing my peace of mind?

📖

To which situations and people do I need to bring peace?

📖

Benedictus *see page 60.*

Our Father

Final Prayer

Let us pray that Christ's peace will find a welcome in the day ahead.

📖

Father, let your family likeness grow in us today.
Deepen the Spirit of Jesus in all we do.
Send us into a world of fragile peace and broken promises,
as signs of hope and of Gospel joy.
Touch our hearts again in the hours ahead,
turning them to thoughts of peace.
Amen

To be repeated often during the day

Peace I leave with you.

✠ **In the name of the Father, and of the Son, and of the Holy Spirit.**

✠ **In the name of the Father, and of the Son, and of the Holy Spirit.**

Greeting

One thing I ask of God,
this is all I need.
To live in God's presence,
every moment of this day.

May I seek God's face
and recognise the goodness of God,
on the journey of this day.

Offering

Father of creation, I offer you this new day of my life. Walk with me through all that will happen. Open my ears to hear your voice guiding my steps. May I walk in a Gospel path and come home tonight with your will done, your Kingdom built up and our friendship forever deepened.
📖

Choral Prayer

Based on Psalm 1:1-3

Blessed are those who do not walk in bitterness
who turn their steps away from anger and pessimism.

Blessed are those who search out God's presence
and uncover the law of love day and night.

They are like trees planted by flowing waters
they will never become hard-hearted or wither in spirit.

They will not be blown about by misfortune
but stay faithfully rooted in God's goodness.

Whatever they do will be drawn into God's wise plan
the fruit of their lives will last forever.

Glory be to the Father...

Meditation

Our life-journey unfolds in mystery, each moment is a gift. Sometimes our day is littered with failure and frustration, sometimes success and surprises overwhelm us with delight. The way of the Christian disciple challenges us to accept both these experiences, as gifts from God. We are called to love and trust both the Cross and the Resurrection, as part of the wisdom of God, who calls us all to be sons and daughters.

The Day Ahead

Does the shadow of the Cross darken any part of the day ahead?
📖
Where is the light of Resurrection likely to shine on my path today?
📖
What challenges do I need to talk to God about, as the day begins?
📖
Where will I find it hard to retain a sense of God's presence?
📖

Benedictus *see page 60.*

Our Father

Final Prayer

Let us pray for peace as this day begins.
📖
Ever-present Father, your watchful care surrounds us completely.
You organise creation so that even the tensions and tragedies of sin never frustrate your loving plans to bring everything to Resurrection.
Help me to embrace your will today,
give me strength to follow your call,
let your truth live in my heart,
to reflect peace to all those I will meet on today's journey.
Amen

To be repeated often during the day

Lord, stay with me on the journey.

✠ **In the name of the Father, and of the Son, and of the Holy Spirit.**

✠ **In the name of the Father, and of the Son, and of the Holy Spirit.**

Greeting

Glory be to God for the gift of this new day.
Glory be to God for light and life.
Glory be to God for time to learn and grow in love.

Guide my thoughts and actions Lord.
Teach me to trust your providence
and accept the gift of this new day with hope.

Offering

Lord, I offer you this day in which your heart and mine can share
all that happens. I offer you all my hopes for this day, and all the
frailty that I bring to life. Speak to my heart in its strength and
weakness. Help me to build your Kingdom of love and justice, in
the hours that lie ahead.
📖

Choral Prayer

Based on Ezekiel 34

I will become the shepherd of my sheep says the Lord
I will seek out the lost and the hidden.

I will rescue them from unhealthy places
to bring them home to their own land.

When they are scattered by the storm
I will gather them together in safety.

I will collect the strays and heal the hurt
I will build up the weak, and guide the strong.

For you are my own flock
I am your Shepherd.

Glory be to the Father…

Meditation

Each day we are shepherded through experiences, both new and old. Like sheep we can follow the crowd and lose touch with the Shepherd, wandering into darkness and danger without the support of a wise guide. As followers of Jesus, we are invited to listen for the voice of the Good Shepherd in our hearts. We are challenged to trust that voice, even when the way leads beyond the understanding of our mind or heart.

The Day Ahead

Where will I hear the voice of the Good Shepherd today?

📖

What will stop me from hearing God's voice?

📖

What dangers, for my peace of mind, lie ahead today?

📖

What do I need to ask of God as the day begins?

📖

Benedictus *see page 60.*

Our Father

Final Prayer

Let us pray for God's guidance in our hearts.

📖

Lord, the love you offer draws us beyond ourselves,
a love exceeding the deepest desires of our hearts,
for you are greater than the human heart.

Guide each thought and action of the day ahead,
so that our frailty and faults may not hide your presence,
but lead us into your providence and peace.
Amen

To be repeated often during the day

The Lord is my shepherd.

✠ **In the name of the Father, and of the Son, and of the Holy Spirit.**

✠ **In the name of the Father, and of the Son, and of the Holy Spirit.**

Greeting

Save us O Lord from cold hearts
and from closed minds,
as a new day begins.

Open us to your love.
May we touch eternity today,
hidden in our ordinary lives.

Offering

Lord, I offer you the journey I make today. May it be woven into your eternal plan of love for all creation. Let me walk alongside others, my eyes wide open to the way your love links our journeys together.

📖

Choral Prayer

Based on Isaiah 43

The Lord says: Do not be afraid, you are my people
we belong together, I have named each one of you.

When you are out of your depth I am still with you
when the waters are rough you will not sink.

Because I am God, you cannot sink beyond my care
I will always sustain you on the journey of life.

So do not be afraid, I am with you each day
I will gather all that has been scattered.

I will bring you home to the heart of God
I made you to be with me forever.

Glory be to the Father...

Meditation

In the Christian tradition, God calls each person individually, but each person is also called into relationship with others. We go to God together. The people of God travel through time, uncovering the mystery of God's presence in their world and handing that mystery on to future generations. It is a shared journey, into the presence of God at the heart of creation. This morning we begin another stage on that journey.

The Day Ahead

With whom will I share the journey of this day?
📖
Who will bring me closer to God today?
📖
Who will need my support to get through the day?
📖
How am I called to live out the Gospel today?
📖

Benedictus *see page 60.*

Our Father

Final Prayer

Let us pray for a greater love of people, made in God's image.
📖
Father, from the days of Abraham until this morning
you have gathered people together,
and shared your presence with them.
Bless your people on this new morning.
May we keep learning how to love each other,
even as you have loved each one of us.
May your love support us whatever we find
in the day that lies ahead.
Amen

To be repeated often during the day

Do not be afraid for I am with you.

✠ **In the name of the Father, and of the Son, and of the Holy Spirit.**

✠ **In the name of the Father, and of the Son, and of the Holy Spirit.**

Greeting
Lord of this morning hour,
Father of light and strength,
today I bring you my poverty and need.

Come into my emptiness,
use my weakness as well as my gifts.
Be a companion through this new day.

Offering
Lord, I offer you this day and all that it will bring. Anchor my day deeply in your presence. Steady my heart and mind, when emotions within and challenges without threaten my peace of mind. Take this day and let your will be done.
📖

Choral Prayer
Based on Jeremiah 31

The people that fled into the desert
have found God's friendship.

Looking for a way to escape
they discovered God searching for them.

So they began to love their God again
building their lives around God's presence.

They were met by God with an everlasting love
an unchanging affection for God's faithful.

In that love they rebuilt their lives together
instead of grumbling quietly they began to sing.

Glory be to the Father...

Meditation

I want it and I want it now has become a mantra of our culture. We are impatient with waiting and emptiness, suspicious of stillness and uncomfortable with silence. Yet, when we are driven into the desert of our own emptiness, we find a God who is always searching for us. In that silence we find that the depth of our emptiness is simply the echo of a love that never ends.

The Day Ahead

Where will I feel most vulnerable during the day?

📖

What will drive me into the empty silence within me?

📖

When will I feel most impatient today?

📖

Where will God be searching for me in the hours ahead?

📖

Benedictus *see page 60.*

Our Father

Final Prayer

Let us pray to be patient with our weakness.

📖

Lord, you know every thought in every mind.
No joy or tear goes unnoticed by your loving care.
Watch over us at the start of a new day,
remind us of the power we have to love,
and the poverty of our spirit.
Open to us today, the hidden treasures of your Kingdom.
Amen

To be repeated often during the day

Blessed are the poor in spirit.

✠ **In the name of the Father, and of the Son, and of the Holy Spirit.**

✠ **In the name of the Father, and of the Son, and of the Holy Spirit.**

Greeting

God loved us so much
that he sent his own Son
to be with us, in the challenges of today.

Lord stay with us in your wisdom,
may this day bring us closer to you
and to each other in your Kingdom.

Offering

Lord of wisdom, I offer you this day, with all my hard-won wisdom
and experience. I offer you the uncertainties and confusion I may
face today. I offer my mixed motives, my fears and my selfishness.
Send your wisdom into all my thoughts, words and actions, so
that, in your wise hands, I may become an instrument of peace
and a source of strength for others. Let your wisdom work in my
weakness.

Choral Prayer

Based on Wisdom 9

Lord, all wisdom comes from you
wisdom that is beyond understanding.

Send that wisdom into our lives
to help us and work with us today.

May wisdom guide our choices
protecting us from folly in our plans.

None of us can understand your plans Lord
we need to trust your wisdom.

It is only in You that we can learn wisdom
through your Spirit that has been sent into our lives.

Glory be to the Father...

Meditation
The life and death of Jesus reveal a wisdom that challenges our view of success and failure. It is a wisdom that often reaches success through failure, a Risen presence that grows stronger in our weakness. When we look at our work and relationships, the same wisdom becomes a challenge of faith. There is wise purpose working within our weakness, God's wisdom of the Cross.

The Day Ahead
Where do I need to ask for God's wisdom today?
📖
How am I likely to experience my weakness during this day?
📖
Who are the wisdom-figures in my life today?
📖
What successes can I look for today?
📖

Benedictus *see page 60.*

Our Father

Final Prayer
Let us pray for the wisdom that goes beyond words.
📖
Father, in Jesus your wise plan became flesh and blood.
Becoming one like us, Jesus has changed our human story
into a relationship of love with a wise and creative God.
As our story unfolds into a perfect love,
help us to trust the Gospel wisdom in the life of the Risen Jesus,
who waits for us at the start of this new day.
Amen

To be repeated often during the day
God chooses what is weak and foolish.

✠ **In the name of the Father, and of the Son, and of the Holy Spirit.**

✠ **In the name of the Father, and of the Son, and of the Holy Spirit.**

Greeting

> God of shyness and subtlety,
> thank you for being with me this morning.
> Uncover your presence in this new day.
>
> Open me, heart and soul, to your Kingdom.
> May I hear your word,
> sifted into the sounds and silences of this day.

Offering

> Lord, thank you for all the anticipation and anxiety with which I
> face this morning. I offer you every thought and word, every event
> and each encounter. May they all find meaning and depth in your
> presence. Let the work I do today be helpful in your plan for a
> better world.
> 📖

Choral Prayer

Based on Luke 13:18

> What is the Kingdom like, to what can I compare it?
> It is like a small mustard seed thrown onto the ground
> that becomes a tree in which the birds can shelter.
>
> The Kingdom of God is like a pinch of yeast
> transforming plain flour into risen bread
> to feed deep and hidden hungers.
>
> Don't always take the easy way out of problems
> enter by the narrow door
> stay focussed on the hidden life of the Kingdom.
>
> Do not let yourselves be separated from God
> nor locked out of the celebration of the Kingdom.
> Do not let your love of God become a thing of the past.
>
> Glory be to the Father...

Meditation

The Christian path leads through loss and failure towards new life. It is a path that is hidden from the clever and calculating, open only to the trusting and child-like spirit. The road to the Kingdom is easily overlooked in the challenges of the day. It is the path towards self-sacrifice, liberating honesty, fragile faith and self-emptying generosity. The path lies hidden in the day ahead, if we have eyes to see it.

The Day Ahead

What would make this day successful for me as a Christian?
📖
What blind spots could put me at odds with God's Kingdom?
📖
Is there a hidden place in my day to find God's presence?
📖
Where will I cross God's path in other people today?
📖

Benedictus *see page 60.*

Our Father

Final Prayer

Let us pray for hope in God's goodness.
📖
Father of all people,
trusting your word is the path to wisdom.
To search for your word is to grow in truth.
Open our eyes to your presence in creation and community.
Open our ears to your call in the day ahead,
so that everything we choose will lead us deeper
into the hidden life you offer your children.
Amen

To be repeated often during the day

The Kingdom of God is among you.

✠ **In the name of the Father, and of the Son, and of the Holy Spirit.**

✠ **In the name of the Father, and of the Son, and of the Holy Spirit.**

Greeting

> Thanks be to God for life and breath,
> for strength to trust,
> for a will to love.
>
> Open my mind and heart Lord
> to all the gifts that lie in wait,
> along the journey of this day.

Offering

> Lord, I make a gift of this day to you. Use my time, my energy and thoughts as you will. I place my life in your hands to use as you wish. Whether this day holds humiliation or success, I offer it all as a small part of your loving plan for the transformation of creation.
> 📖

Choral Prayer

Based on Matthew 7:13

> Don't always take the easy way out
> there are no short-cuts to God.
>
> Try to enter by the narrow way of self-denial
> by the hard road of committed trust in God.
>
> Be slow to trust others as guides for the journey
> judge them by what they are and not by what they say.
>
> It is not those who have the right words that matter
> but the ones who do the Father's will.
>
> Those who listen and follow the Father's will
> build their lives on an eternal foundation.
>
> Glory be to the Father…

Meditation

God asks simply that we do our best in living a spiritual life. When we have planted and watered, let us not forget that it is God alone who can make things grow. For that reason we need to learn to wait on the providence of God. If we seem to be making no progress at all, let us maintain our peace of mind. Let us leave the abundance of the harvest to the Lord.

St Francis de Sales

The Day Ahead

What expectations do I bring to the day?

How will I trust in God's providence today?

How will I choose the narrow and challenging path today?

Benedictus *see page 60.*

Our Father

Final Prayer

Let us pray for trust in God.

Father, open our eyes to everyday blessings.
Deepen our trust in your constant presence in life.
May friendship with you become the foundation
of an eternal relationship with all creation.
Bring us closer to your Kingdom of justice and peace today.
Amen

To be repeated often during the day

I place all my hope in you Lord.

✠ **In the name of the Father, and of the Son, and of the Holy Spirit.**

✠ **In the name of the Father, and of the Son, and of the Holy Spirit.**

Greeting

Thanks be to God for creation and new life.
Thanks be to God for time to grow and change.
Thanks be to God ever old and ever new.

Father thank you for a new day,
for all its uncertainty and routine patterns.
It is the place where you and I will work together.

Offering

Lord, I offer you my life today with its mixed motives and plans for the hours ahead. Take my heart and purify my motives, take my mind and clarify my plans. Make me a good and faithful servant of your Kingdom in all that happens.

📖

Choral Prayer

Based on Luke 16:10

The one who is trusted in little things
will be trusted with greater responsibility.

The one who is dishonest in small things
will never be trusted with what really matters.

If a person cannot be trusted with ordinary things
who would trust them with genuine riches?

No one can satisfy the demands of two masters
you cannot be the slave of both God and money.

It is too easy to act the part of a virtuous person
God reads the heart and knows the truth about us all.

Glory be to the Father…

Meditation

The inner spirit is never free from the outer culture in which it lives. There is a daily tension between the demands of an outer world of the possible, and the demands of an inner world of hopes and ideals. The first can lead to superficiality, and the second to unrealistic hope and disappointment. The Gospel liberates us from both disappointment and superficiality, by putting a relationship with the Father at the centre of each life. This relationship grows deeper as it meets disappointment and emptiness. This experience is the way of the Cross.

The Day Ahead

How will I be tempted to serve another god today?

What motives lie behind my plans for the day?

Where do I need to challenge other values today?

Where will I deepen my relationship with God?

Benedictus *see page 60.*

Our Father

Final Prayer

Let us pray to the God of freedom and new life.

Father, words cannot contain the mystery of your love.
Lift us beyond the limitations of measured lives
to the eternal reach of your loving kindness,
uncovered in the Death and Resurrection of Jesus.
Set us free to live and love in the same Spirit
that moved Jesus to give his life for others.
Amen

To be repeated often during the day

Lord, you know my heart and my mind.

✠ **In the name of the Father, and of the Son, and of the Holy Spirit.**

✠ **In the name of the Father, and of the Son, and of the Holy Spirit.**

Greeting

> Lord of life and love,
> thank you for this new day,
> gifted to us by your kindness.
>
> Lord of challenge and change,
> stay with us in all that happens
> in the day that lies ahead.

Offering

> Lord, I offer you this day with all the generosity I have. I give you
> each hour, each decision and each challenge. Help me to choose
> the path of love today. Whether it be in compassion or in
> challenge, may I learn to do the most loving thing. May I ease the
> pain and injustice of the world and help to build your Kingdom
> today.
> 📖

Choral Prayer

Based on Luke 6:27

> Love your enemies
> do good to those who hurt you.
>
> Bless those who curse you
> pray for those who treat you badly.
>
> Give to everyone who asks
> do not chase the one who robs you.
>
> Treat others as you would wish to be treated
> you will be children of your Father in heaven.
>
> Love your enemies, do good to those who hurt you
> your reward will be great in heaven.
>
> Glory be to the Father...

Meditation
The Gospel is about recognising God's presence and doing God's will, in generous self-sacrificing love. Christians certainly need to develop their personal gifts, but the motivation is not self-fulfilment, but self-emptying. The love that liberates is not self-love, but the love that dares to give meaning to death, by growing through emptiness, into an eternal relationship with God.

The Day Ahead
What patterns of selfishness will I tend to slip into today?
📖
Where will I be called upon to turn the other cheek?
📖
Where will my generosity be tested?
📖
Who are my enemies today?
📖

Benedictus *see page 60.*

Our Father

Final Prayer
Let us pray for the strength that comes from God's love.
📖
Father, we thank you for the trust that binds us together,
aware that selfishness can tear us apart.
Keep us united in the love that gives meaning to our lives,
help us to draw encouragement from the Gospel we follow.
Amen

To be repeated often during the day

Love your enemies.

✠ **In the name of the Father, and of the Son, and of the Holy Spirit.**

✠ **In the name of the Father, and of the Son, and of the Holy Spirit.**

Greeting

Father of Creation,
thank you for this newly created day,
to be shared in your presence.

Father, may I be with you today,
as fully as you move in my heart and mind
at the beginning of this new day.

Offering

Lord, I offer you today the air that I breathe, the water I wash with,
and my energy to move in your world. Keep me open to the way
your presence is moving in my day. Like air and water help me to
bring freshness and inspiration to all the challenges I meet today.
📖

Choral Prayer

Based on Luke 12:35

Be dressed and ready to get into action.
Don't let the darkness cloud your mind.

Be like a door-keeper
waiting to open up when the master comes home.

If you are ready to welcome the master
you will be treated as a friend and companion.

Those who stay awake will recognise danger
and not allow violence to enter their home.

Stand ready and be watchful
the Lord will come at a time you do not expect.

Glory be to the Father...

Meditation

God's love cannot be contained, because it is alive and flowing, through all life. When we open our heart to what is life-giving, we become aware of this flow. Then, like a doorkeeper, we can open our lives to an eternal love, flowing in time.

The Day Ahead

How do I feel as I begin this day?

📖

Am I ready to be sensitive and flexible today?

📖

Where am I in touch with life and energy this morning?

📖

What attitudes and memories may block my life and love today?

📖

Benedictus *see page 60.*

Our Father

Final Prayer

Let us pray to the Father whose love keeps us safe.

📖

Lord, help us to recognise you as the source of creation,
a loving Father at the heart of each person.
Teach us to cling to your promises in an uncertain world.
Keep us safe in your peace and secure in your love,
as we share your work of creation today.

Amen

To be repeated often during the day

Lord, let your love flow through me today.

✠ **In the name of the Father, and of the Son, and of the Holy Spirit.**

✠ **In the name of the Father, and of the Son, and of the Holy Spirit.**

Greeting

Thank you Lord for the dawn of a new day,
for the gift of light and life.
Thank you for vision and purpose to guide my steps.

Lord of light stay with me today,
enlighten my doubts and desires,
shine through my choices today.

Offering

Lord, I offer you my hopes and fears today. I offer you the light and
shadows within me. Let me walk in the light of your presence all
day. May your light shine through me clearly that others will
recognise your goodness in me. May I never hide your light in the
way I live today.

📖

Choral Prayer

Based on Matthew 6:22

The eye opens the whole body to the light
good eyes fill a person with light.

A damaged eye will bring shadows and uncertainty
filling a life with darkness.

If the light within a person becomes dark
how can that person ever trust what they see?

How is it that you can see a splinter in another's eye
and ignore a plank in your own?

Do not judge and you will not be judged
because the judgements you hand out
will be the ones you receive yourself.

Glory be to the Father...

Meditation

We are called to be children of the light, open, playful, honest and dependent upon God. Darkness creeps into our lives when we forget to play, when we choose isolation and take ourselves too seriously, as independent people. We are not made for independence. We are made to belong to a loving Father. We are children of the light, not of darkness. Our hearts are restless, until we recognise our dependence on God.

The Day Ahead

What shadows are there inside me as the day begins?

📖

Where will lightness and truth be most accessible today?

📖

Who will need the light of my presence today?

📖

Where will I find darkness a threat?

📖

Benedictus *see page 60.*

Our Father

Final Prayer

Let us pray for strength to turn away from darkness.

📖

Father of all creation,
in Jesus, your light has broken into our lives.
Through the Cross and Resurrection,
your love has been uncovered as the heart of the universe.
Guide us by that Gospel light today.
Lighten our hearts with your truth today.
Amen

To be repeated often during the day

The Lord is my light.

✠ **In the name of the Father, and of the Son, and of the Holy Spirit.**

✠ In the name of the Father, and of the Son, and of the Holy Spirit.

Greeting

Lord, open my mind and heart this morning,
to see the world through your eyes,
and act as you would wish throughout this day.

Help me to speak the truth in kindness,
admit mistakes honestly,
and give my time generously in this new day.

Offering

Lord, I offer you this unused day. I offer all the enthusiasm but also
the reluctance I feel for what lies ahead. Be with me in my fears,
to calm my mind. Be with me in success and surprises, to help
me celebrate. Be with me in the silence, to deepen my love for
you today.

📖

Choral Prayer

Based on Luke 12:1

Be on your guard against hypocrisy
for everything that is hidden will eventually be uncovered.

What you have said in secret will be brought into the light of day
what you have whispered quietly will be shouted out loud.

Do not fear what can only harm the body
fear instead what can harm your friendship with God.

No one is beyond God's friendship and loving kindness
every hair of your head has been counted.

Even a sparrow is not forgotten in God's sight
you are worth much more than sparrows.

Glory be to the Father…

Meditation

As a Christian, I do not need to fill my life with noise, busyness or many people. At times it is good to stop and let the dust of activity settle: to know what I will find in the silence. At first there may be some disappointment and restlessness, but beneath, there is more: gratitude for life itself, humour at my own silliness, compassion for suffering and a quiet wisdom distilled from a spirit-filled life. God's truth is never far away.

The Day Ahead

Where will I find it hard to be honest today?

How will I find space for stillness?

Do I feel that I am worth more than many sparrows?

How will I be a sign of God's loving kindness for others?

Benedictus *see page 60.*

Our Father

Final Prayer

Let us pray for enthusiasm in serving others.

Father, in the Resurrection of your Son,
death became a doorway to new life.
His courage and faith have opened up a new age of hope.
Let us never drift back into old ways,
or be content with empty promises and short-lived success.
Keep us close to you today, make our happiness holy,
and all our love, life-giving for others.
Amen

To be repeated often during the day

The truth will set you free.

✠ **In the name of the Father, and of the Son, and of the Holy Spirit.**

✠ **In the name of the Father, and of the Son, and of the Holy Spirit.**

Greeting

Thank you Lord, for another opportunity,
a chance to live another day in your presence,
a chance to share your life with others.

Thank you Lord for your word,
sown in my heart and history.
May it find deeper roots in my life today.

Offering

Lord, I offer you my life and all my understanding. I offer my anxiety, distractions and everything I value in the day that lies ahead. Let your word take root in my fragile life. Through my actions, may your word produce wisdom and kindness, to be broken open and shared with all those I meet today.
📖

Choral Prayer

Based on Matthew 13:18

Those who hear the word without understanding
find that word carried away from their hearts.

Those who allow the word little depth in their lives
soon find that it is uprooted in time of trouble.

Those who receive the word without trust
allow anxiety and worry to stifle its goodness.

Those who do not welcome the word as a treasure
are likely to devalue it in their daily living.

Those who hear, welcome and act on the word
produce a rich harvest of life and truth for many people.

Glory be to the Father...

Meditation

If you really want to reach God and want that desire summarised in just one little word, here is your answer: the word is *Love*. Fasten this word firmly to your heart, so that it never leaves you. Whatever befalls you, cling to this word in your heart. If any other thoughts press themselves upon you to ask what you want or need, you have the answer in this little word, *Love*.

The Cloud of Unknowing - 14th Century English mystic.

The Day Ahead

What distractions might lie ahead for me today?

Where will cares and worries stifle a sense of God's presence?

Where will I be able to draw on experience and wisdom?

Where will I find depth and stillness today?

Benedictus *see page 60.*

Our Father

Final Prayer

Let us pray that we will be faithful to the light we have received.

Father, surrounded as we are by uncertainty,
let the light of your truth guide us
deeper into your Kingdom today.
Help us to trust the Gospel you have given to us.
Let your love form us all into the family you have called us to be.
Amen

To be repeated often during the day

The harvest is great and labourers few.

✠ **In the name of the Father, and of the Son, and of the Holy Spirit.**

✠ **In the name of the Father, and of the Son, and of the Holy Spirit.**

Greeting

> Thank you Lord, for this morning,
> for the fading stars and the rising sun,
> calling me back into action in your world.
>
> Thank you for another chance
> to share in the mystery of your life-giving love,
> at the heart of creation.

Offering

> Lord, I offer you my heart today. May I remain in touch with my feelings and in touch with you. Show me the road that leads deeper into the story of Cross and Resurrection. Move my heart today into the way of service and compassion. Help me to recognise your invitations to share in your self-sacrificing love for others.
> 📖

Choral Prayer

Based on Matthew 20:17

> We are travelling towards Jerusalem
> to the city of the Cross and Resurrection.
>
> To a place of rejection mockery and death
> towards struggle, and conflict with authority.
>
> You know authority usually makes itself felt
> it likes to maintain its own greatness.
>
> If you want to be great you should become a servant
> only then will you grow into the Kingdom of God.
>
> The Son of Man came not to be waited upon
> but to pour out his life in the service of many people.
>
> Glory be to the Father...

Meditation
When we move the focus of our lives from our own needs to the needs of others, liberation is achieved. A force is set free inside us that can transform lives. That force is genuine love and for those who receive it, unmistakable. When we want possessions, people or knowledge, just for ourselves, we block the flow of love and compassion in the world and everyone suffers as a result.

The Day Ahead
How do I feel about the day ahead?
📖
Where do I feel empty, where do I feel enriched?
📖
How will I use the power of love and compassion today?
📖
How will I handle authority today?
📖

Benedictus *see page 60.*

Our Father

Final Prayer
Let us pray for an increase in compassion in the human heart.
📖
Lord, let the goodness of your life continue to grow in us.
Draw us deeper into the life-giving process of change.
Teach us the wisdom of the Cross and Resurrection.
Help us to overcome injury and injustice.
Increase our compassion for those who suffer.
Amen

To be repeated often during the day
Greatness comes through service.

✠ **In the name of the Father, and of the Son, and of the Holy Spirit.**

✠ **In the name of the Father, and of the Son, and of the Holy Spirit.**

Greeting

Lord, thank you for the touch of your hand,
waking me from sleep,
helping me to start the day.

Thank you for my frailty and needs,
leading me to rely more on you
than on my own independence.

Offering

Lord, I offer you this day and invite you to share it with me. Touch
my day with your hand. Guide all my actions, my thoughts and my
feelings. May I recognise each touch of your hand today. Give me
the trust and the courage to respond when you invite me into
action or to stillness.

📖

Choral Prayer

Based on Matthew 18:1

Who is most important in God's Kingdom?
The one who becomes as open and trusting as a child.

Unless you change and become like a child
you will not be able to grow into God's Kingdom.

Whoever recognises their own frailty and needs
will be most important in God's eyes.

Those who realise and welcome their dependence
welcome God's presence into their lives.

Those who avoid their own frailty and emptiness
will also miss God in their experience.

Glory be to the Father...

Meditation

The basic characteristic of childhood is dependence, finding strength in others and relying upon it. As Christians, we are called to dependence, to a kind of vulnerability to others and to God. A vulnerability which is life-giving. Independence is not our natural state. We are made for one another, to search out the meaning of life and love, together with other people. The image of the child reminds us that our frailty and dependence are vital signposts on the path to truth and life.

The Day Ahead

Who will I be happy to depend upon today?

📖

Where will I resent being dependent?

📖

Who will need to depend upon me today?

📖

When will I find time, like a child, to play?

📖

Benedictus *see page 60.*

Our Father

Final Prayer

Let us pray for the gift of recognising God's presence.

📖

Lord, open our eyes to see you in the beauty of creation,
and in the mystery of each fragile human life.
This world is holy because it is touched by your hand.
Touch our lives this morning with your loving kindness,
so that we can share this day with each other
in self-giving and service.
Amen

To be repeated often during the day

Whoever welcomes a child in my name, welcomes me.

✠ **In the name of the Father, and of the Son, and of the Holy Spirit.**

✠ **In the name of the Father, and of the Son, and of the Holy Spirit.**

Greeting

> Lord, thank you for finding me
> in these quiet moments,
> before I begin the day.
>
> Help me to find you
> and recognise you calling my name,
> in today's rhythms and routines.

Offering

> Lord, I offer you my day. Help me to see the paths and pitfalls that lie ahead. Be with me, as a shepherd, to guide and protect me every hour. Open my ears to your call to do what is loving and wise. Give me the courage to recognise and accept the help you offer on the day's journey. Make me ready to support others, in your way of love today.
> 📖

Choral Prayer

Based on Matthew 18:12

A shepherd owned one hundred sheep
and one of them was lost.

He left the ninety-nine safe in the fold
and went to find the stray.

The shepherd found more delight in the stray
than in the ninety-nine who never left the fold.

As it was with the shepherd in the hills
so it is with Jesus the Shepherd of our souls.

Jesus delights in bringing to the Father
those who are far from their home.

Glory be to the Father...

Meditation

Our culture is more concerned with productivity than community. There is a temptation to busyness, rather than being. Our self-worth is tied too closely to achievement rather than to our dignity, as human beings. For Christians, those who are weak, under-achieving, dependent and difficult, become signs of a deeper dignity. Their need reminds us of our own frailty, they call us home to a more honest relationship with God and one another.

The Day Ahead

Today, what am I likely to close my ears to?
📖
What kind of distractions will I have to manage today?
📖
Where will my patience be challenged today?
📖
How will I find time to listen for God's word?
📖

Benedictus *see page 60.*

Our Father

Final Prayer

Let us pray for a kindness that never fails.
📖
Lord, you shower us with gifts each day.
Each life is an eternal gift from your love.
Shepherd our lives in your loving kindness today,
for only your love can make us whole and bring us home.
May the generous sharing of our gifts and needs
reveal your path of love in the day ahead.
Amen

To be repeated often during the day

I am the Good Shepherd I know my sheep.

✠ **In the name of the Father, and of the Son, and of the Holy Spirit.**

✠ **In the name of the Father, and of the Son, and of the Holy Spirit.**

Greeting

Thank you God, for all that will happen today,
for all the surprises and sameness
that will make this day unique.

Thank you for gathering up each event
and drawing it into your plan
of Cross and Resurrection to new life.

Offering

Lord, I offer you my day, my unique experience of your life and
love. Take this day and my reactions to all that happens. Help me
to co-operate with your inspirations, and shoulder the crosses
that come to me, on the way to a deeper love for life and people
today.

📖

Choral Prayer

Based on Matthew 25:34

Come to me you who have been blessed by my Father
receive the Kingdom for which you were made.

For I was starving and you gave me food
I was thirsty and you gave me a drink.

I was a refugee and you made space for me
I was naked and you clothed me.

I was sick and you nursed me
in prison and you visited me.

Lord, when did we see you thirsty or naked?
When did we see you a refugee or in prison?

In so far as you helped any of my brothers and sisters
you helped me, says the Lord.

Glory be to the Father...

Meditation
The birds of the air have a nest to escape to in their need. A stag has a thicket to hide in, to avoid the heat or the hunters. Our own hearts need a place to escape to briefly during the day. It may be a picture of the Cross, or an image of the wounds of Christ, which put our struggles into a wider context of purpose and meaning. There is a strength and wisdom in this kind of practice.

St Francis de Sales

The Day Ahead
In whom will I find it easy to see God's goodness today?
📖
In whom will it be difficult to see God's goodness?
📖
When will I need to escape and be still for a short time?
📖
What cross do I need to shoulder today?
📖

Benedictus *see page 60.*

Our Father

Final Prayer
Let us pray to be signs and bearers of God's love for others.
📖
Father, renew us in spirit this morning.
Touch our lives again with your presence, living in people.
Help us to grow in your family likeness.
May we share your goodness
with our brothers and sisters, wherever we meet them
during this newly created day.
Amen

To be repeated often during the day

I was hungry and you gave me food.

✠ **In the name of the Father, and of the Son, and of the Holy Spirit.**

✠ **In the name of the Father, and of the Son, and of the Holy Spirit.**

Greeting
Risen Lord, you breakfasted by the lake
with your disciples.
Be with me as I start my day.

In ordinary moments,
in meals and in meetings,
may I recognise your Risen presence.

Offering
Lord, I offer you this day. Help me live out your challenge to love
You and my neighbour in everything that happens. Give me a
glimpse of your goodness in creation and in the words and faces
of all those I meet in the day ahead.
📖

Choral Prayer
Based on Mark 12:28

The first commandment is this,
there is one God of all creation
who is to be loved with heart and soul and strength.

The second commandment is this,
you must love one another
with as much strength as you love yourself.

To love God with heart, understanding and strength
is more important than rituals and detailed rules.

To love your neighbour as you love yourself
is more important than any pious prayers.

Those who live these words in their lives
are close to the Kingdom of God.

Glory be to the Father...

Meditation

It is so easy to claw back or compartmentalise our Christian commitment. We become selective about our love of God and our love of neighbour. In doing this, prejudice and self-interest undermine the generosity of our first commitment to the Gospel. It is easy to smuggle back into our hearts the values of a selfish world. Each day is a challenge, to re-commit ourselves to radical service of God and neighbour. I must be ready to start again today.

The Day Ahead

How will I show love for my neighbour today?
📖
During this day, when will I find space for God?
📖
How will I show respect for myself and others today?
📖
Who in my circle of awareness needs my prayer and help?
📖

Benedictus *see page 60.*

Our Father

Final Prayer

Let us pray humbly and hopefully before our God.
📖
Loving Father, your love goes beyond all boundaries.
Your care embraces the whole of creation.
May the barriers of prejudice
and the abyss of ignorance that divide us,
be bridged by your love and goodness,
living in ordinary people.
Amen

To be repeated often during the day

Love your neighbour as yourself.

✠ **In the name of the Father, and of the Son, and of the Holy Spirit.**

✠ **In the name of the Father, and of the Son, and of the Holy Spirit.**

Greeting

> Thank you Lord for the hours that lie ahead,
> whatever they hold.
> I know I will share them all with you.
>
> Thank you Lord, for the partnership we live each day.
> I will find strength to do the right thing
> and a truth that lasts forever in that sharing.

Offering

> Lord, here is my day. I gather all my thoughts about the day ahead, my hopes and fears, and I put them in your hands. In the course of today may I reach out for your hand in peace and in panic. May we meet the day together so that I can grow in love and honesty with others.
> 📖

Choral Prayer

Based on Mark 4:35

> Leaving the crowd Jesus got into a boat with his disciples
> a great storm began to threaten their crossing.
>
> Jesus was alone in the stern, tired-out with work
> his head was on a cushion, he was fast asleep.
>
> The disciples woke him with frantic fear
> amazed at his calmness in the fierce storm.
>
> Jesus woke up and spoke to the wind and the sea
> a great calm settled around them all.
>
> Jesus asked the disciples to rise above their fears
> through trusting their Father in heaven.
>
> Glory be to the Father...

Meditation
Lord, when Pilate asked you what is truth, you refused to answer. The truth is not just facts, but relationships and meanings. Each experience in life is an unfolded truth, a part of the pattern of meaning and relationships that leads us deeper into our own lives and purpose. The truth is not something we hold. You are the Truth, who takes hold of us, and makes us sons and daughters of God.

The Day Ahead
What aspect of truth do I need to focus on today?
📖
What storms of life do I anticipate in the day ahead?
📖
What memories will help and hinder my plans today?
📖
How will I renew my trust in God throughout the day?
📖

Benedictus *see page 60.*

Our Father

Final Prayer
Let us pray for truth and integrity in our lives.
📖
Lord, you are the source of all truth,
everything comes together in your plan for life.
Help us to hear your word in every sound we hear,
and be patient as your truth emerges in our lives.
In all the uncertainties of a changing world,
help us to cling to you, Lord, more than to life itself.
Amen

To be repeated often during the day

Why are you afraid, where is your faith?

✠ **In the name of the Father, and of the Son, and of the Holy Spirit.**

✠ **In the name of the Father, and of the Son, and of the Holy Spirit.**

Greeting

> Lord of inspiration,
> move in my life today,
> and help me do your will.
>
> Lord of peace and forgiveness,
> be with me to build bridges,
> to forget the pain of the past.

Offering

> Lord, I offer you this day with all it may bring. I offer you my awareness of your presence, let it grow deeper today. I offer you the fears that come from past failure, help me to distil wisdom from experience. I offer you my trials and temptations, may they bring me closer to you today.
> 📖

Choral Prayer

Based on Mark 1:9

Jesus came from Nazareth to the river Jordan
and was baptised in the river by John.

The skies were torn open above Jesus
and the Spirit descended on him in the form of a dove.

This is my beloved Son, a voice declared from heaven
my love and friendship rest on all he does.

The same Spirit drove Jesus into the desert
to be alone and to be tested for forty days.

Jesus was with the wild beasts
and angels looked after him.

Glory be to the Father…

Meditation
Many people think that because they feel bad about themselves, God is far away and unhappy with them. They assume that God is only interested in happy and successful people. In fact God is with us in all our moods. We believe in a Gospel that recognises the importance of failure, isolation, suffering and even death, as key points in finding a deeper relationship with God. God slips through the cracks in our emotional lives, to deepen a relationship, that will heal us and last forever.

The Day Ahead
Do I feel God's favour rests upon me this morning?

📖

What moods seem to isolate me from God's presence?

📖

Where will I be tested in the day ahead?

📖

Where will I be invited into quietness today?

📖

Benedictus *see page 60.*

Our Father

Final Prayer
Let us pray to the God who forgives and gives new life.

📖

Lord, source of everything that is good,
give us the will to please you in the day ahead.
Open our minds to the ways your love works,
so that we might become wise in our weakness,
and grow stronger in trusting you today.
Amen

To be repeated often during the day

I am God's beloved.

✠ **In the name of the Father, and of the Son, and of the Holy Spirit.**

✠ **In the name of the Father, and of the Son, and of the Holy Spirit.**

Greeting

Peace in this morning light.
Peace to all those I will meet today.
Peace to anyone I will think about today.

Lord I accept the gift of this day with a peaceful heart.
Help me to keep peaceful in mind and heart today,
whatever happens.

Offering

Lord, I offer you today the power I have to love others. Make my
love balanced and generous. Help me to be fair and honest, but
also kind and forgiving, in the way I express care and concern.
Make this day another lesson in loving like you, with generosity,
justice and mercy.
📖

Choral Prayer

Based on 1 John 4:7

Let us love one another
because love comes from God.

Everyone who loves with generosity
is already caught up into the love of God.

God has made the first move in this love
by sending Jesus to close the gap between God and humanity.

Since God has come close to us in love
we should love each other and overcome our differences.

No one has ever seen God
but if we live in love we share God's own Spirit.

Anyone who lives a loving life
lives in God and God in them.

Glory be to the Father...

Meditation
The love that we see in Jesus is full of warmth and concern, His heart went out to people very easily. It was also a love that challenged, courageously naming hypocrisy and refusing to be manipulated by others. It was a love in which justice and mercy met, in a liberating and disturbing way. This is the kind of generous, trusting, love that is the model for all Christian relationships.

The Day Ahead
Am I beginning this day at peace?

📖

Where am I challenged by justice today?

📖

Where will my heart go out to others in compassion today?

📖

Where will I need to make the first move in mercy or justice?

📖

Benedictus *see page 60.*

Our Father

Final Prayer
Let us pray for justice and mercy in our world.

📖

Lord, in you, mercy and justice have embraced.
You have created us out of love,
every day you draw us into the eternal circle of your life.
Help us to share our lives in both mercy and justice,
so that we may not be hard-hearted.
Challenge us to grow in the discipline of your self-giving love.
Amen

To be repeated often during the day
Love comes from God.

✠ **In the name of the Father, and of the Son, and of the Holy Spirit.**

✠ **In the name of the Father, and of the Son, and of the Holy Spirit.**

Greeting

Thank you for the dawn of a new day,
the birth of new hope,
the beginning of a new chapter in God's love.

May I breathe in the newness of today
and breathe out those habits of mind and heart,
that diminish my power to love others.

Offering

Lord, I offer you my day, balanced between the person I was
yesterday and the person I wish to be today. Help me to keep
growing in awareness of you, and not cling to fears and false
dreams. Make this day a step towards the freedom of a heart
renewed in the service of others.

📖

Choral Prayer

Based on John 14:23

If you love me you will become like me
the Father will make a home in your heart.

The Spirit will teach you everything
keeping the Gospel alive in your actions.

Peace I leave with you
peace that comes from trusting the Father.

Do not be anxious or afraid
we are only separated for a short time.

I am going to join the Father
but I shall return and take you with me.

Glory be to the Father…

Meditation

Poverty of spirit and simplicity of heart are often under-valued in modern culture. Being street-wise and self-contained are much more highly prized. Simplicity often cuts through the confusion of life, leading to peacefulness of heart. Poverty of spirit involves a mutual dependence that can enrich relationships. Remembering our need can make us free in spirit and able to love others as Christ loves us. God chooses what is weak and foolish to confound our plans and bring us back to love.

The Day Ahead

Am I open to learning from what might happen today?

📖

Can I recognise my needs as opportunities to trust?

📖

Where will I find the peace that Christ promised?

📖

How can I live as a daughter or son of God today?

📖

Benedictus *see page 60.*

Our Father

Final Prayer

Let us pray for peaceful and dependent hearts.

📖

Father, help us to trust that you are with us,
in the muddle and confusion of our lives.
May we recognise our poverty today and give us a simple heart.
Teach us to look after one another peacefully,
and keep us focussed on the call to serve as Jesus did.
May we learn to be true sons and daughters
of our Father in heaven.

Amen

To be repeated often during the day

Do not be anxious or afraid.

✠ **In the name of the Father, and of the Son, and of the Holy Spirit.**

✠ **In the name of the Father, and of the Son, and of the Holy Spirit.**

Greeting
Lord of the morning,
give me life and energy
to begin this day well.

Take my strength and weakness
and let it become a witness today,
to your hidden presence in our world.

Offering
Lord, I offer you my strength, to be a witness to the Gospel today.
I offer you my weakness, to give me a deeper trust in your
presence in my life. I offer you all the opportunities I will have to
challenge attitudes that do not lead to your love and compassion
for all people.
📖

Choral Prayer
Based on John 15:18

If the world rejected me it will also reject you too
because we do not belong to this kind of world.

If you did belong to the world as it is today
you would be happy with its injustice and coldness.

But because I have called you out of that world
you will be at odds with it and a challenge to it every day.

I tell you this so that you will not be disturbed by troubles
and be ready to stand for the love that brings life.

I will send you the Spirit
to confirm and strengthen your witness to the Gospel.

Glory be to the Father...

Meditation

The radical nature of the Gospel is often weakened by repetition in church and compromises in Christian action. Loving enemies, sharing property, the closeness of God and the dignity of each person, these put Christians at odds with many aspects of our present culture. There should be a struggle each day between Christians and the world they live in. I am called to continue that struggle today.

The Day Ahead

Where do I need to stand my ground today?

📖

Do I see anger as a possible call to action from God?

📖

What aspects of my world am I at odds with today?

📖

How do I recognise the Spirit in my own life-experience?

📖

Benedictus *see page 60.*

Our Father

Final Prayer

Let us pray for a love-based law in our world.

📖

Father, justice is only perfected when founded on love.
Help us to deal with each other lovingly today,
even when we are hurt or angry.
May we act with justice, and not let revenge affect our choices.
Help us support a law of love that names and challenges
all that is not just in our relationships and in society.
Amen

To be repeated often during the day

Stand for the love that brings life.

✠ **In the name of the Father, and of the Son, and of the Holy Spirit.**

✠ **In the name of the Father, and of the Son, and of the Holy Spirit.**

Greeting

Thank you Lord for another day of experience.
May I never take for granted
the gift of time, to learn and love in your world.

Thank you for the lessons this day will bring
and the opportunity to know myself better
and recognise your presence.

Offering

Lord, I offer you all the words that will cross my mind and my lips
today. May they be truthful, tactful and touched with your creative
love. Use my words and actions to add to the amount of loving
kindness in the world. Make me ready to work to build a better
world.

Choral Prayer

Based on John 1

From the beginning there was the Word
the Word was with God, the Word was God.

Everything that exists came to be through the Word
and was marked with the Word's own life.

That life of God's Word
is the light of all people.

The Word was the true light
that revealed the human heart and mind.

It is a light that overcomes darkness
enlightening the hearts and minds of all people.

Glory be to the Father...

Meditation
Our God is a God of history, present in and through whatever happens. The daily struggles between friends, the political squabbles of governments and the search for knowledge, are all areas where God's presence and plans are at work. The Kingdom, described in the Gospel, emerges through ordinary events and not in a separate sacred space. Our God gets involved actively in the world, through us. We are called again to that partnership today.

The Day Ahead
Where do I need light in the day ahead?

Who needs my forgiveness today?

Where is God calling me to partnership for the Kingdom today?

Where will my hope and trust feel most fragile today?

Benedictus *see page 60.*

Our Father

Final Prayer
Let us pray for the peace of the Kingdom.

Father, you give us time to learn from experience,
and begin each day a little wiser in your love.
Help us to extend this forgiving love to others today,
so that we might build our relationships
on hope and trust in your Kingdom among us.
May the beauty of this forgiving love unfold in us today.
Amen

To be repeated often during the day

I am the light of the world.

✠ **In the name of the Father, and of the Son, and of the Holy Spirit.**

✠ **In the name of the Father, and of the Son, and of the Holy Spirit.**

Greeting

Lord, thank you for my life today.
Thank you for my body and mind,
my gifts and my story so far.

Thank you for revealing your presence
in the flesh and blood of Jesus.
Reveal your life in my flesh and blood today.

Offering

Lord, I offer you my body, with all its strengths, aches and pains.
I offer you my mind and the dreams and hopes it contains. Take
my life today, body and soul, and let it become a sign of your
presence in the world.
📖

Choral Prayer

Based on John 1

The Word was made flesh in this world
and was not recognised.

The Word entered the world
and was rejected by God's own people.

But all who could accept the word
found that they were children of God.

The word became flesh like us
and lived alongside us.

We saw the grace of God's presence
revealed in flesh and blood.

Glory be to the Father...

Meditation

Many Christians see the flesh as a dangerous source of temptation and weakness. They are right, at least in part. However the Gospel suggests that the flesh is also the place where we meet God. In the passion and the fragility of our flesh, God breaks into our lives. In human compassion for each others' weakness, we also touch the forgiveness of God. In the passion of the flesh, we touch the joy and energy of a creator God. Our flesh has been transformed through faith, into a pathway to God's presence.

The Day Ahead

How does my body feel about a new day?

Am I taking care of myself in both body and soul?

Who needs my energy and passion today?

Where is gentleness and compassion needed today?

Benedictus *see page 60.*

Our Father

Final Prayer

Let us pray for courage to live the questions of life.

Father, the mystery of your presence overwhelms us.
Your goodness is beyond the touch of our hearts,
and your strength escapes the reach of our minds.
Give us courage to seek the mystery of your presence
in the experience of living and the intuitions of faith.
Amen

To be repeated often during the day

The Word was made flesh.

✠ **In the name of the Father, and of the Son, and of the Holy Spirit.**

✠ **In the name of the Father, and of the Son, and of the Holy Spirit.**

Greeting

Thanks be to God for life,
for it's mystery unfolding in time,
for it's meaning in my own story.

Thanks be to God for the chance to serve,
to grow in wisdom today,
to love with a sincere heart.

Offering

Lord, I offer you this new day. I offer you my plans, knowing that they might go wrong in many ways. Stay with me during the day and help me to adapt and change my plans according to your plan of love and justice. Help me to live this day with a sincere and sensitive heart.
📖

Choral Prayer

Based on 1 Thessalonians 4:14

Be at peace among yourselves
and give encouragement and strength to one another.

Warn those who are lazy to care for the weak
give courage to the worried be patient with everyone.

Don't let arguments linger on
nor let them spill over into revenge and coldness.

Try to do what is best for others in family and friends
and strive to be happy and cheerful every day.

Turn your mind and heart to God's presence regularly
and give thanks for all that happens.

Glory be to the Father...

Meditation
In our rush to achieve more, we may be blinded by ingratitude to what has already been achieved. A grateful heart recognises and names goodness, wherever it is found. What we take for granted, slips through our hands. What we take for granted in ourselves, may be lost as a source of grace. There is a God-given energy in gratitude, that is part of the rhythm of each day. We need to be thankful for the start of this day.

The Day Ahead
Where will I need to be most positive and grateful today?
📖
How will loving kindness touch my day?
📖
How will I serve others and allow others to care for me?
📖
Where am I likely to make a fool of myself?
📖

Benedictus *see page 60.*

Our Father

Final Prayer
Let us pray for sincerity of heart.
📖
Lord, you catch each moment of our day,
and in loving kindness give meaning to every event.
Travel with us on the journey of this day
support us in doing good and protect us from foolishness.
Help us to share your loving kindness
by a life of sincere service to others.
Amen

To be repeated often during the day

Give thanks for all that happens.

✠ **In the name of the Father, and of the Son, and of the Holy Spirit.**

✠ **In the name of the Father, and of the Son, and of the Holy Spirit.**

Greeting

Father of creation,
open my eyes to a new day
and your presence hidden within this new beginning.

Take away the anxious fears that linger.
Give me courage to hope
and strength to love.

Offering

Lord, I offer you my day. I offer you the fears that sometimes haunt
my heart. May my fear become an opportunity to trust you more
and learn my limitations. Open my eyes to the ways in which you
turn a challenge into a new chance, and a failure into faithfulness.
Help me to live this day in the logic of your love.
📖

Choral Prayer

Based on Romans 8:14

Everyone who is moved in heart or mind by the Spirit
is a daughter or a son of God.

This is not a Spirit of slavery or manipulation
it is a spirit of free choice inherited by God's own children.

The whole of creation shares this journey towards freedom
it aches and groans in waiting to be set free.

The Spirit comes to help us in our waiting weakness
connecting us to God in a way deeper than words.

God lives with each person in love
turning everything to their eternal good.

Glory be to the Father...

Meditation

We are, as Christians, a Resurrection people. We believe that tombs are temporary resting-places. We can live a very different reality in our daily thoughts and plans. We tell ourselves that we will never overcome some problem or issue. We tell ourselves that some people are beyond help or forgiveness. We believe in Resurrection, but we live at times, among the tombs of disappointment. Let the light of Resurrection shine into our lives today.

The Day Ahead

What am I looking forward to in the day ahead?

📖

Who do I need to praise and thank today?

📖

Where am I called to trust?

📖

Where am I challenged by change?

📖

Benedictus *see page 60.*

Our Father

Final Prayer

Let us pray for calm and clear hearts.

📖

Lord, your presence supports us all day long,
and searches out what is best within us.
Take away the fear that hides us from your sight.
Remove our blindness to your presence,
folded into the twists and turns of each day.
Amen

To be repeated often during the day

The Spirit waits for us in our weakness.

✠ **In the name of the Father, and of the Son, and of the Holy Spirit.**

Benedictus

Blessed be the Lord
who comes, today, to set us free.

Our liberation has arrived
from within our own experience.

We have been set free from frustration
as the prophets had foretold.

God's promises have been fulfilled
and we are sanctified.

For there is a Child given to us
to be with us on the road.

God's tender mercy, like the morning sun,
rolls back the darkness of our lives.

We walk with God, out of the shadow of death
side-by-side, in the way of peace.

Glory be to the Father...